VOCAL SELECTIONS

Stacey Mindich

Mickey Liddell   Hunter Arnold   Caiola Productions   Double Gemini Productions
Fakston Productions   Roy Furman   Harris Karma Productions
On Your Marks Group   Darren Bagert   Roger & William Berlind
Bob Boyett   Colin Callender   Caitlin Clements   Freddy DeMann   Dante Di Loreto
Bonnie & Kenneth Feld   FickStern Productions   Eric & Marsi Gardiner   Robert Greenblatt
Jere Harris and Darren DeVerna   The John Gore Organization   Mike Kriak   Arielle Tepper Madover
David Mirvish   Eva Price   Zeilinger Productions   Adam Zotovich   Ambassador Theatre Group
Independent Presenters Network AND The Shubert Organization

EXECUTIVE PRODUCERS
Wendy Orshan and Jeffrey M. Wilson

IN ASSOCIATION WITH
Arena Stage   Second Stage Theatre
Molly Smith, Edgar Dobie   Carole Rothman, Casey Reitz

DEAR EVAN HANSEN

BOOK BY   MUSIC AND LYRICS BY
STEVEN LEVENSON   BENJ PASEK & JUSTIN PAUL

STARRING
BEN PLATT

LAURA DREYFUSS   RACHEL BAY JONES
JENNIFER LAURA THOMPSON   MIKE FAIST   MICHAEL PARK
WILL ROLAND   KRISTOLYN LLOYD

SCENIC DESIGN BY	PROJECTION DESIGN BY	COSTUME DESIGN BY	LIGHTING DESIGN BY	SOUND DESIGN BY
DAVID KORINS	PETER NIGRINI	EMILY REBHOLZ	JAPHY WEIDEMAN	NEVIN STEINBERG

HAIR DESIGNER	MUSIC DIRECTOR	MUSIC COORDINATORS	VOCAL ARRANGEMENTS & ADDITIONAL ARRANGEMENTS BY
DAVID BRIAN BROWN	BEN COHN	MICHAEL KELLER MICHAEL AARONS	JUSTIN PAUL

ADVERTISING	PRESS REPRESENTATIVE	DIGITAL MARKETING	MARKETING PARTNERSHIPS
SERINO COYNE	DKC/O&M	SITUATION INTERACTIVE	ROSE POLIDORO

CASTING BY	PRODUCTION MANAGEMENT	PRODUCTION STAGE MANAGER	COMPANY MANAGER
TARA RUBIN CASTING LINDSAY LEVINE, C.S.A.	JUNIPER STREET PRODUCTIONS	JUDITH SCHOENFELD	KATRINA ELLIOTT

ASSOCIATE DIRECTOR	ASSOCIATE PRODUCERS	GENERAL MANAGER
ADRIENNE CAMPBELL-HOLT	JAYNE HONG RACHEL WEINSTEIN	101 PRODUCTIONS LTD.

MUSIC SUPERVISION, ORCHESTRATIONS
& ADDITIONAL ARRANGEMENTS BY
ALEX LACAMOIRE

CHOREOGRAPHY BY
DANNY MEFFORD

DIRECTED BY
MICHAEL GREIF

Originally presented by Arena Stage – July 9, 2015 to August 23, 2015
New York premiere at Second Stage – March 26, 2016 to May 29, 2016

Cover art courtesy of Serino Coyne

ISBN 978-1-4950-9167-4

HAL•LEONARD®
7777 W. BLUEMOUND RD. P.O. BOX 13819 MILWAUKEE, WI 53213

Visit Hal Leonard Online at
www.halleonard.com

SPECIAL THANKS TO:

Dror Baitel

Jon Balcourt

Brian Barone

Josephine Bearden

Haley Bennett

Ben Cohn

Nicholas Connors

Daniel Gittler

Khiyon Hursey

Christopher Jahnke

Paul Staroba

Enrico de Trizio

Scott Wasserman

Ian Weinberger

ANYBODY HAVE A MAP?

Music and Lyrics by BENJ PASEK
and JUSTIN PAUL
Vocal arrangements by Justin Paul
Piano arrangement by
Alex Lacamoire and Justin Paul

Slightly awkward (♩ = 108)

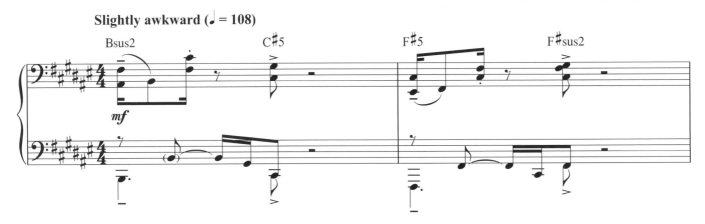

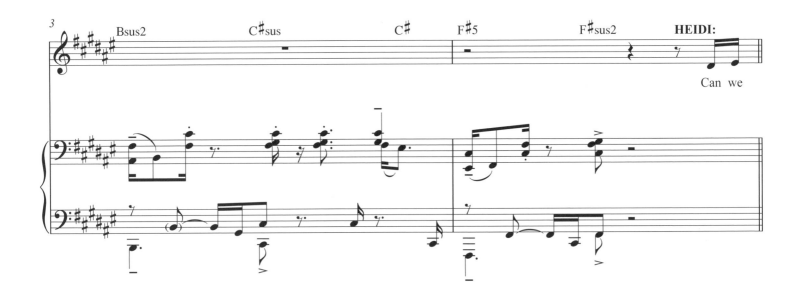

HEIDI:
Can we

try to have __ an op-ti-mis-tic out-look? Can we

WAVING THROUGH A WINDOW

Music and Lyrics by BENJ PASEK
and JUSTIN PAUL
Vocal arrangements by Justin Paul
Piano arrangement by
Alex Lacamoire and Justin Paul

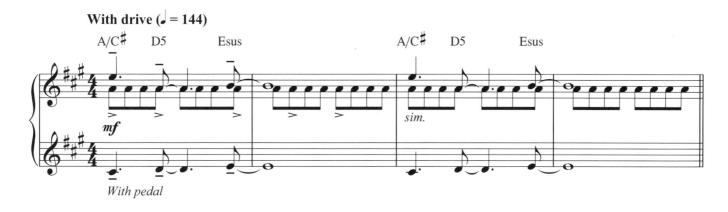

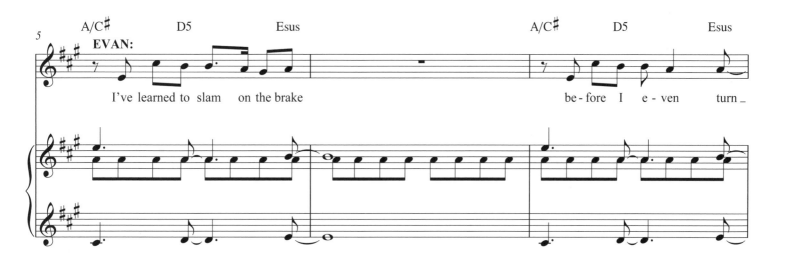

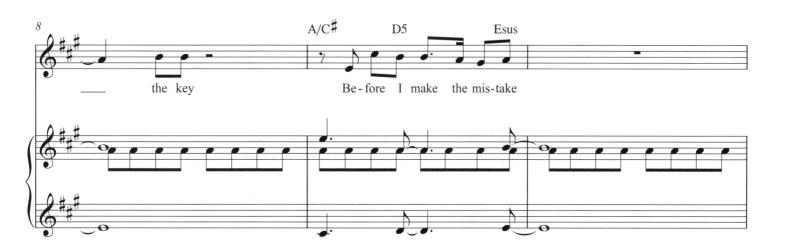

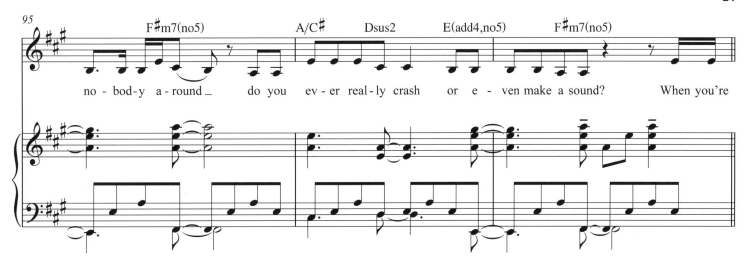

no-bod-y a-round __ do you ev-er real-ly crash or e-ven make a sound? When you're

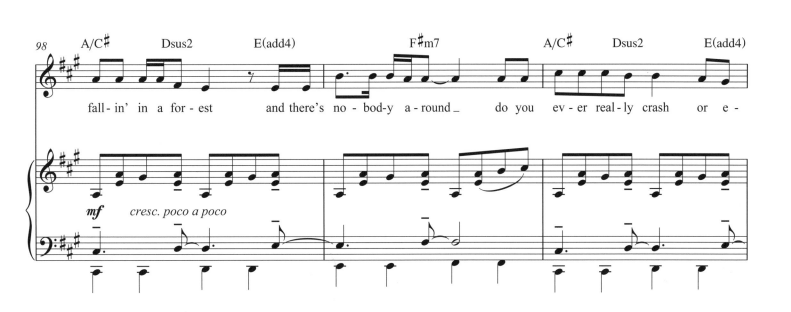

fall-in' in a for-est and there's no-bod-y a-round __ do you ev-er real-ly crash or e-

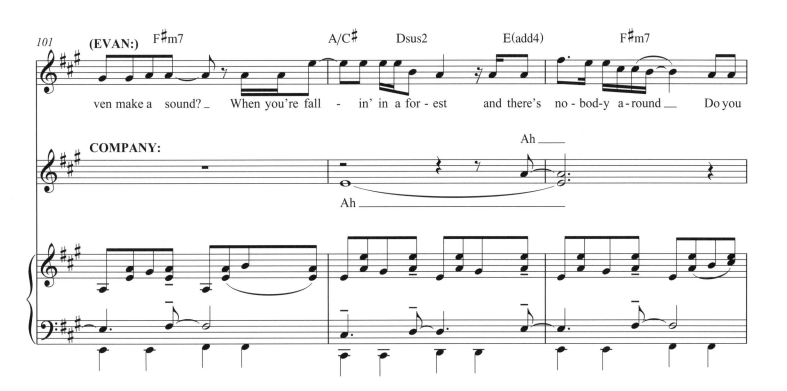

(EVAN:) ven make a sound? __ When you're fall - in' in a for-est and there's no-bod-y a-round __ Do you

COMPANY:

Ah ____

Ah ____

FOR FOREVER

Music and Lyrics by BENJ PASEK
and JUSTIN PAUL
Vocal arrangements by Justin Paul
Piano arrangement by
Alex Lacamoire and Justin Paul

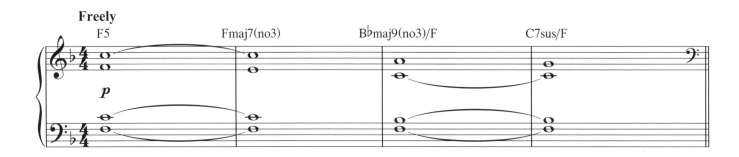

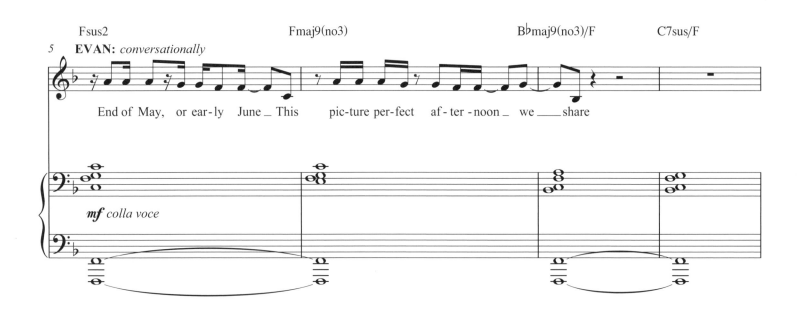

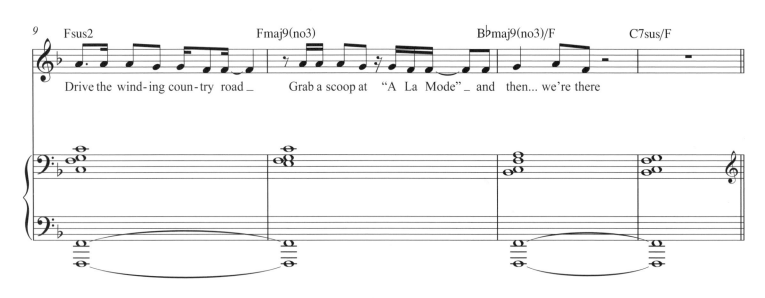

With pedal

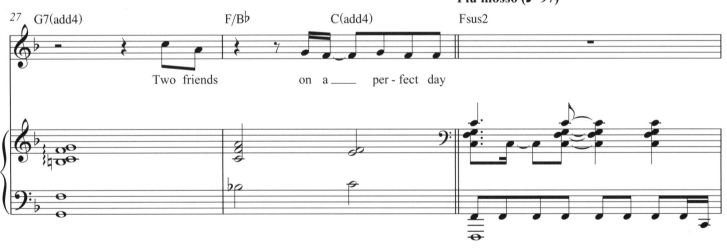

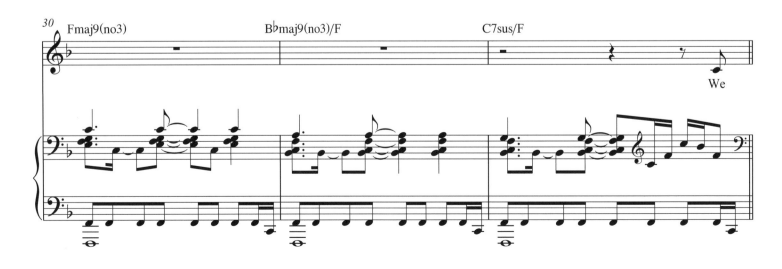

SINCERELY, ME

Music and Lyrics by BENJ PASEK
and JUSTIN PAUL
Vocal arrangements by Justin Paul
Piano arrangement by
Alex Lacamoire and Justin Paul

Upbeat Piano Rock, Swing 8ths (♩ = 196)

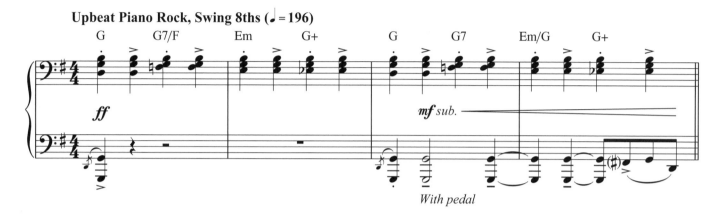

CONNOR:
Dear Ev-an Han-sen: We've been way ___ too out of touch

Things have been cra-zy And it sucks ___ that we don't talk ___ that much

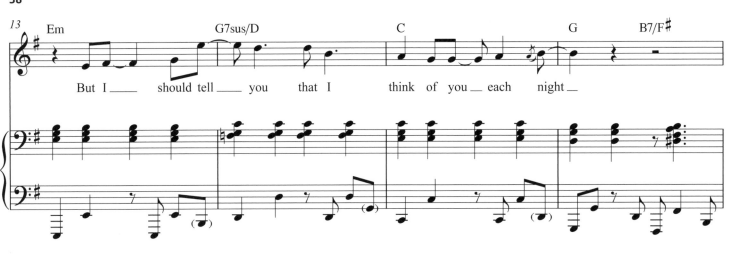

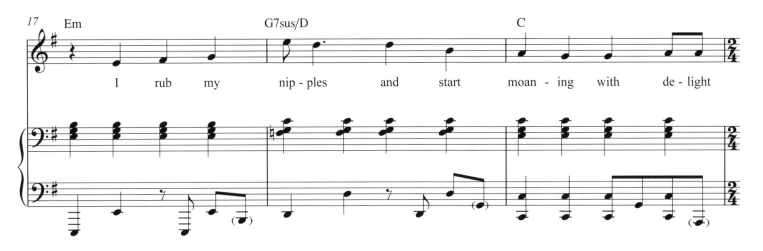

(in the clear)
EVAN: *Why would you write that?*
JARED: *I'm just trying to tell the truth.*
EVAN: *This needs to be perfect. These emails have to prove that we were actually friends. Just...I'll do it.*

(GO ON)

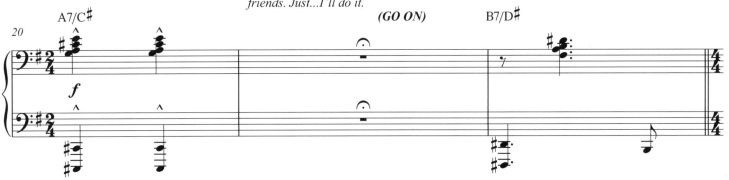

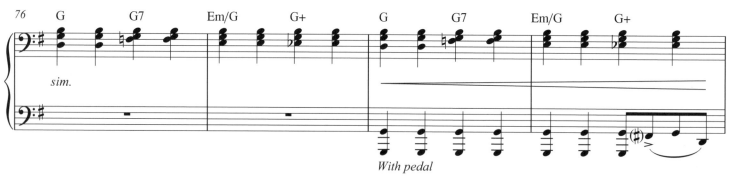

REQUIEM

Music and Lyrics by BENJ PASEK
and JUSTIN PAUL
Vocal arrangements by Justin Paul
Piano arrangement by
Alex Lacamoire and Justin Paul

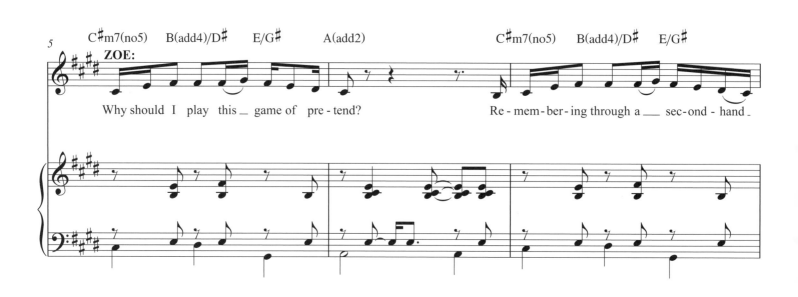

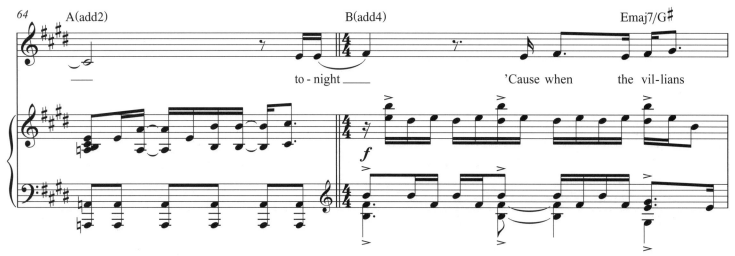

IF I COULD TELL HER

Music and Lyrics by BENJ PASEK
and JUSTIN PAUL
Vocal arrangements by Justin Paul
Piano arrangement by
Alex Lacamoire and Justin Paul

EVAN: *He thought you were...awesome.*
ZOE: *He thought I was "awesome." My brother.*
EVAN: *Definitely.*
ZOE: *How?*
EVAN: *Well...*

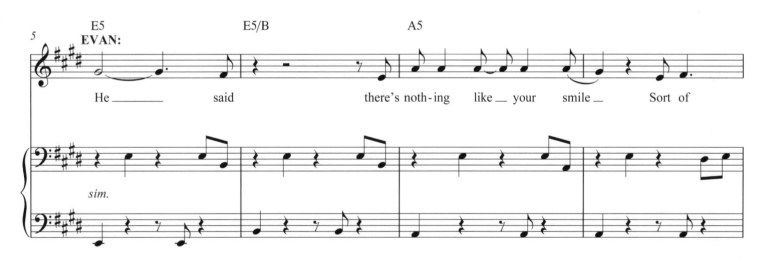

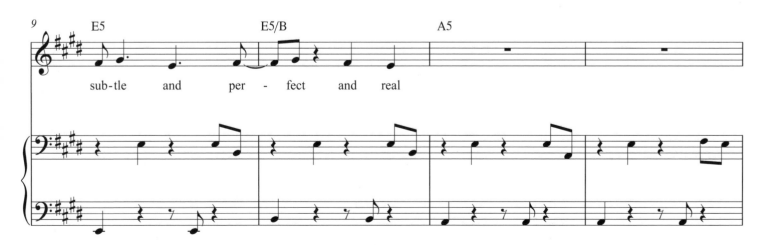

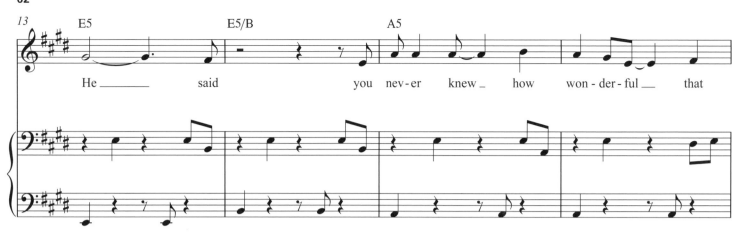

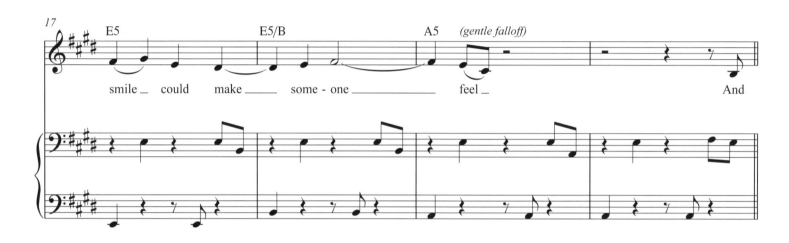

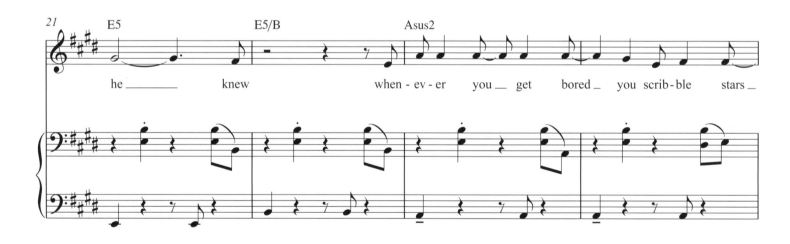

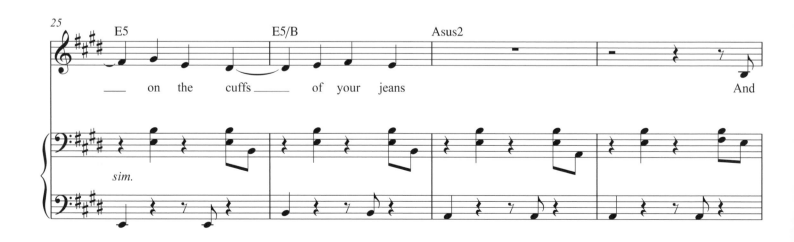

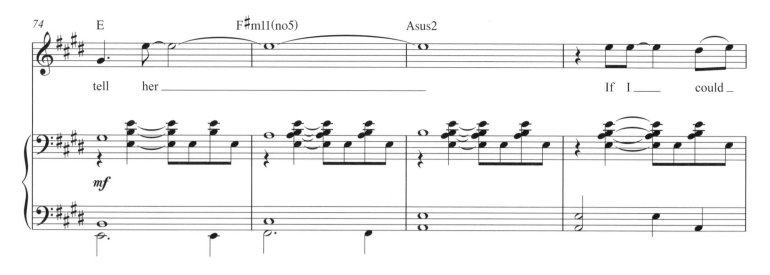

tell her ____ If I ___ could _

tell her" ____

ZOE: *Did he say anything else?*
EVAN: *About you?*
ZOE: *Never mind. I don't even really care anyway...*

EVAN: *No no no, he said so many things, I'm just...trying to remember the best ones.*

DISAPPEAR

Music and Lyrics by BENJ PASEK
and JUSTIN PAUL
Vocal arrangements by Justin Paul
Piano arrangement by
Alex Lacamoire and Justin Paul

Freely, conversational

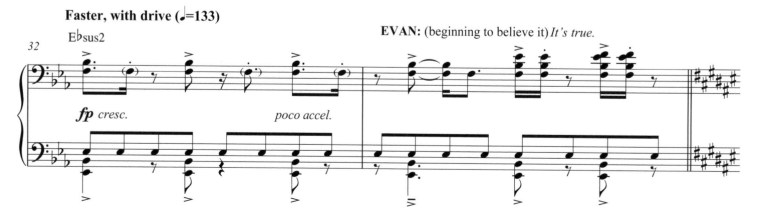

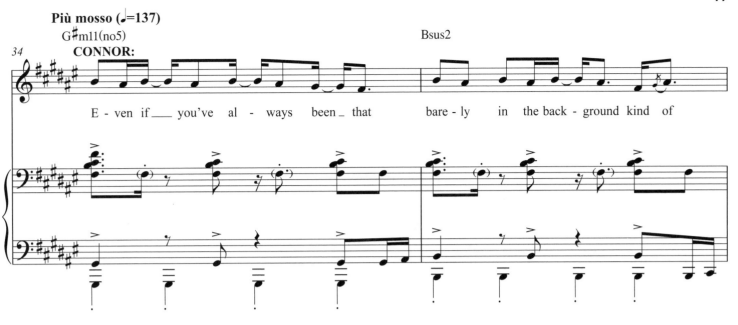

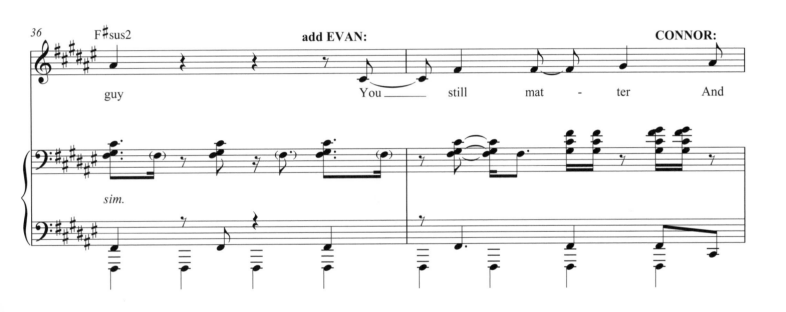

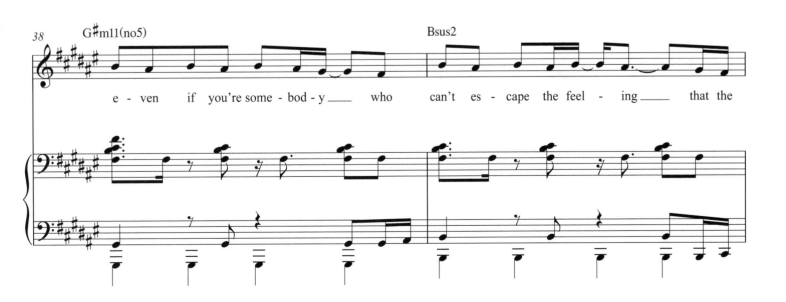

worlds passed ___ you by   If you

EVAN:

You ___ still mat - ter

nev - er get a - round to do - ing some re - mark - a - ble thing ___

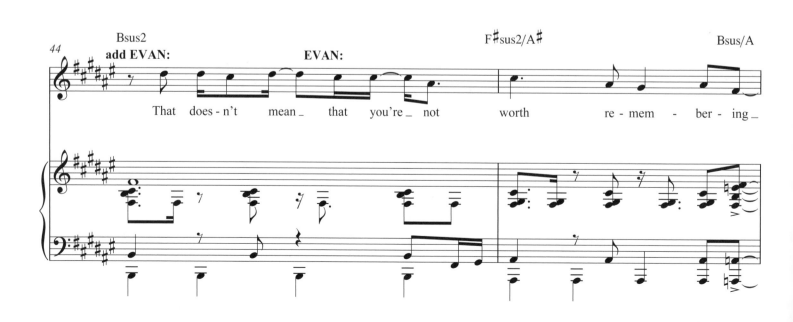

add EVAN: EVAN:

That does - n't mean ___ that you're ___ not   worth   re - mem - ber - ing ___

bod-y to find ___ you You're fall-in' in a for-est and when you hit ___ the ground ___

All you need ___ is for some-bod-y to find ___ you

EVAN: *I'm calling it the Connor Project.*
JARED: *The Connor Project.*
EVAN: *A student group dedicated to keeping Connor's memory alive, to showing that everybody should matter.*

ALANA: *We have to do this. Not just for Connor. For everyone.*

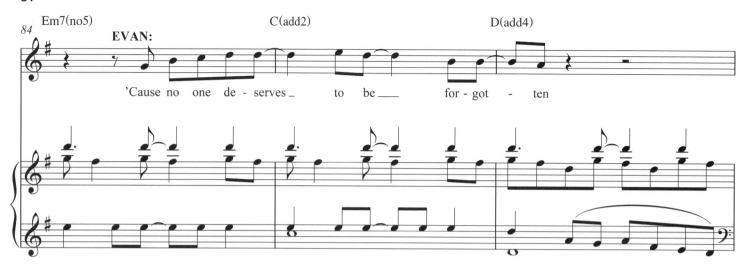

'Cause no one de - serves_ to be_ for - got - ten

ALANA: No one de - serves_ to fade_ a - way_

JARED: No one de - serves_ to fade_ a - way_

EVAN: No one de - serves_ to fade_ a - way_

EVAN: *We're calling it the Connor Project.*
CYNTHIA: *The Connor Project.*
EVAN: *Imagine a major online presence.*
JARED: *A massive fundraising drive...*
ALANA: *And for the kickoff event...*

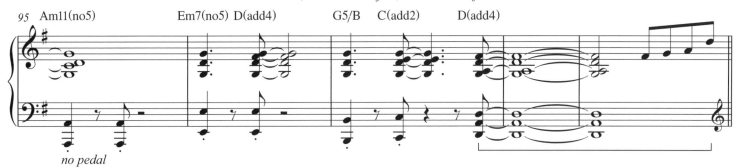

ALANA (cont'd):*...an all-school memorial assembly.*
LARRY: *I didn't realize that Connor meant this much to people.*
CYNTHIA: *Oh, Evan...this is just, this is wonderful.*

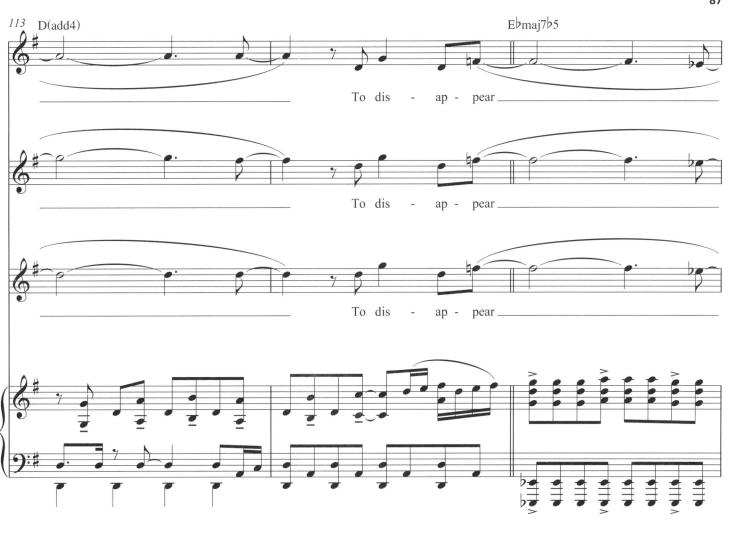

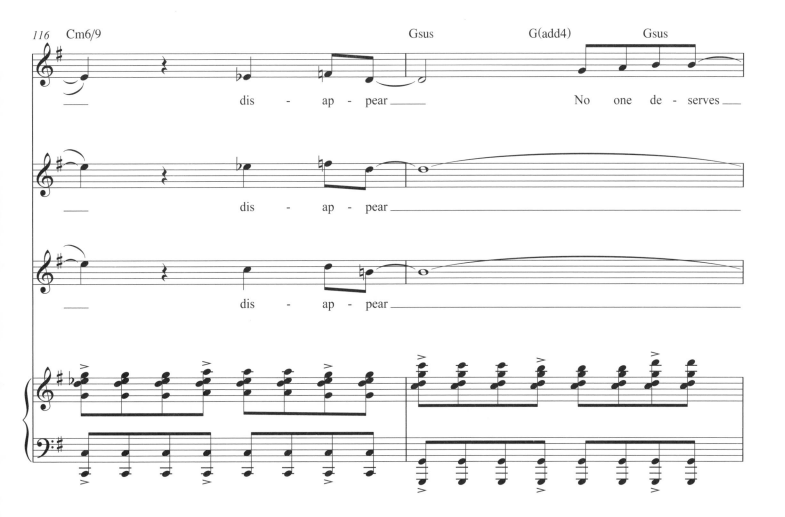

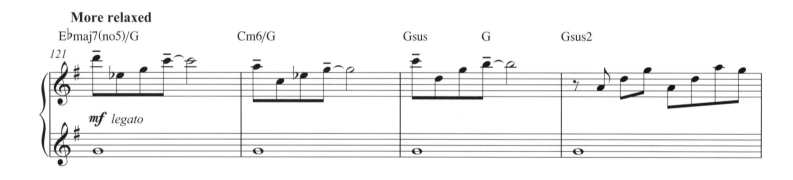

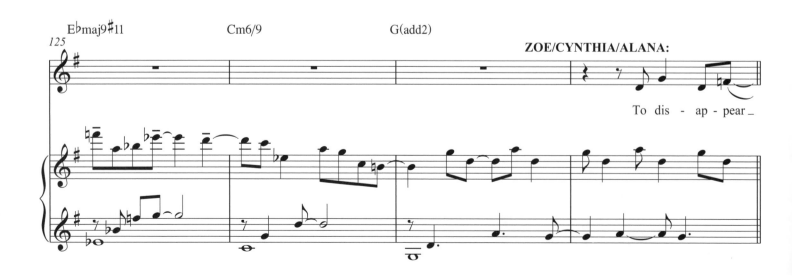

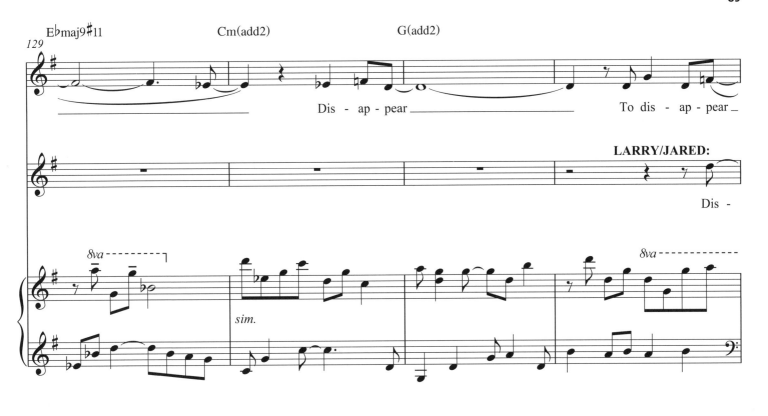

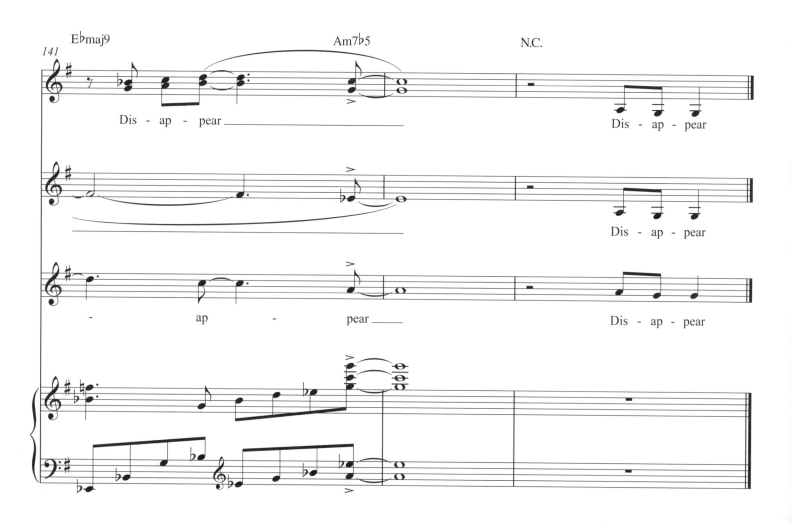

YOU WILL BE FOUND

Music and Lyrics by BENJ PASEK
and JUSTIN PAUL
Vocal arrangements by Justin Paul
Piano arrangement by
Alex Lacamoire and Justin Paul

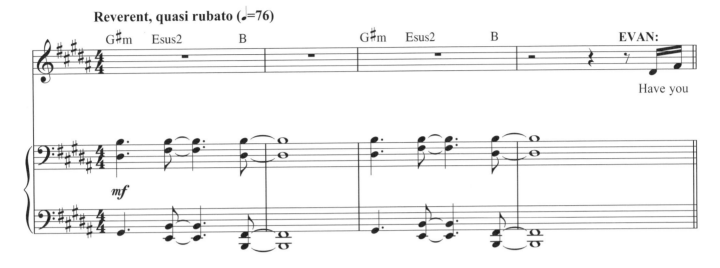

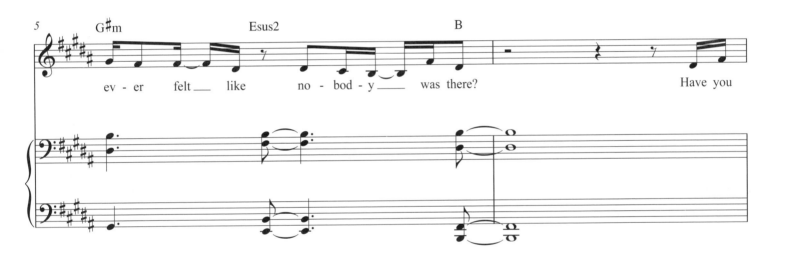

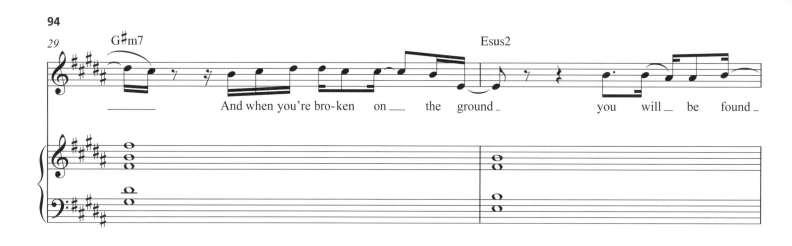

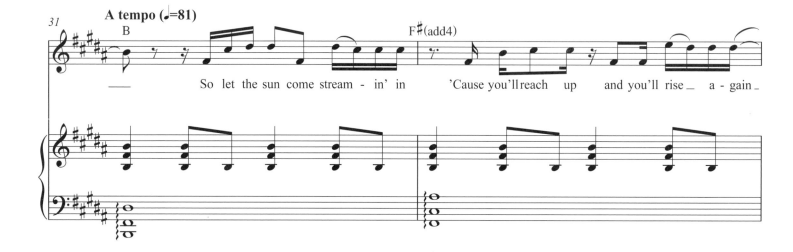

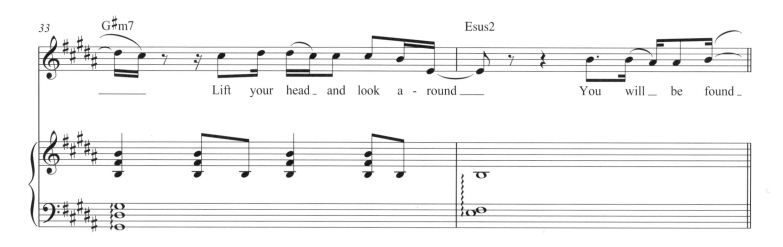

ALANA: *Have you seen this? Someone put a video of your speech online.*
EVAN: *My speech?*

ALANA: *People started sharing it, I guess, and now,*
I mean, Connor is everywhere.
JARED: *Your speech is everywhere.*

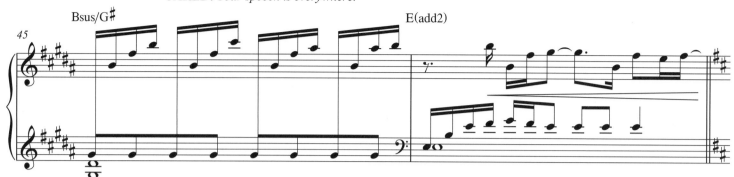

JARED: (con't) *This morning, the Connor Project page,*
it had fifty-six people following it.
EVAN: *How many does it have now?*
JARED: *Four thousand, five hundred, and eighty-two.*

CYNTHIA (overlapping with **JARED**):
Sixteen thousand, two hundred,
and thirty-nine.

EVAN: *I don't understand. What happened?*

CYNTHIA: *You did.*

ALANA:

There's a

VIRTUAL COMMUNITY:
Oh my God
Everybody needs to see this

place ___ where we don't have ___ to feel ___ un - known

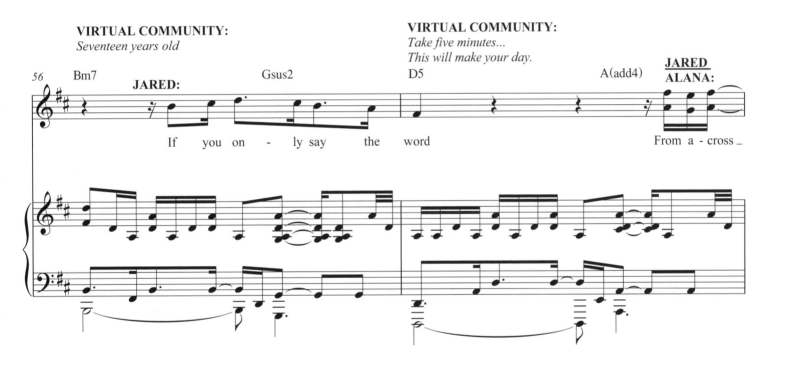

VIRTUAL COMMUNITY:
Share it with the people you love
Re-Post
The world needs to hear this
A beautiful tribute
Favorite

COMPANY & VIRTUAL COMMUNITY:

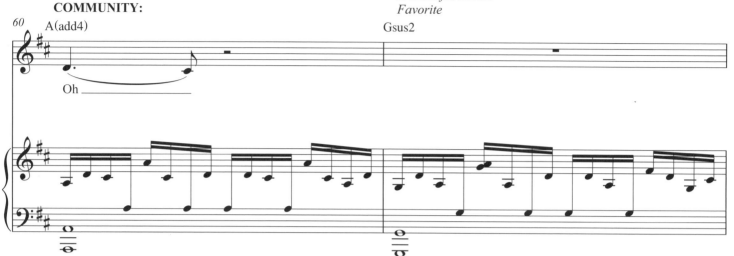

VIRTUAL COMMUNITY:
I know someone who really needed to hear this today. So thank you, Evan Hansen, for doing what you're doing

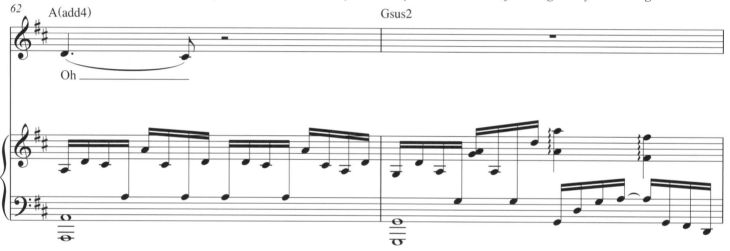

VIRTUAL COMMUNITY:
I never met you, Connor. But coming on here, reading everyone's posts...
It's so easy to feel alone, but Evan is exactly right...

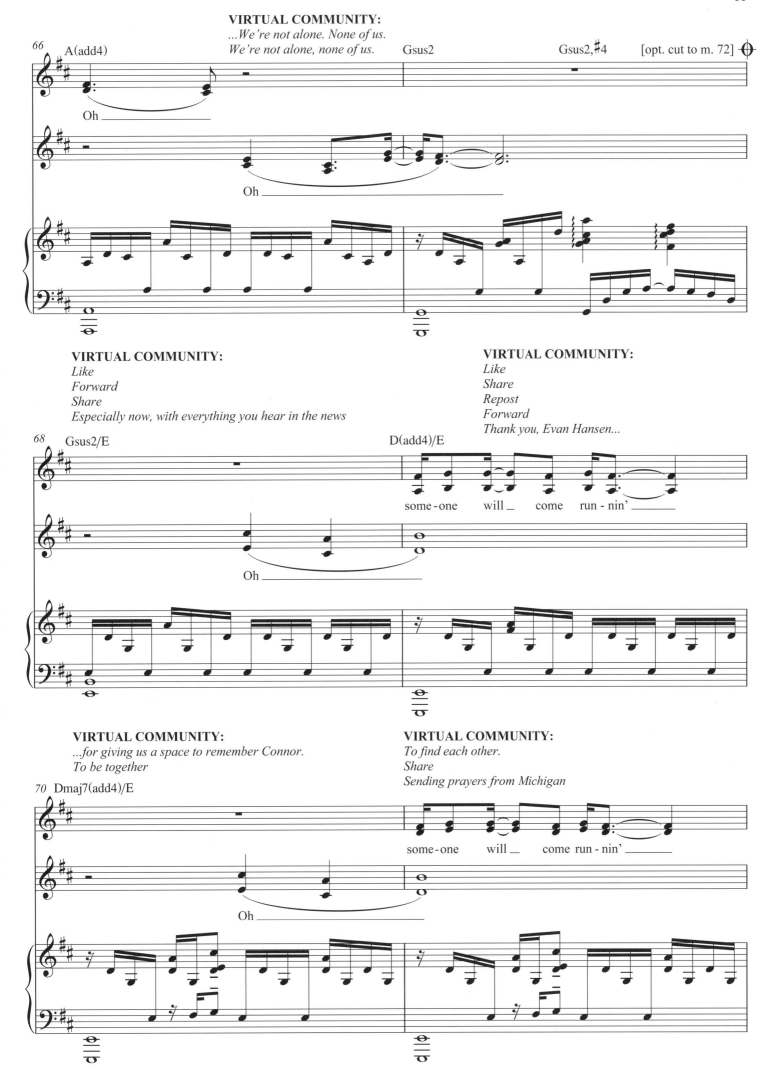

VIRTUAL COMMUNITY:
Vermont
Tampa
Sacramento
Thank you, Evan Hansen

VIRTUAL COMMUNITY:
Re-Post
Thank you, Evan
Watch until the end
Thank you, Evan Hansen

VIRTUAL COMMUNITY:
This video is everything right now
Thank you, Evan Hansen
Thanks to Evan
All the feels
Thank you, thank you

VIRTUAL COMMUNITY:
This is about community
The meaning of friendship
Thank you, Evan
Evan Hansen

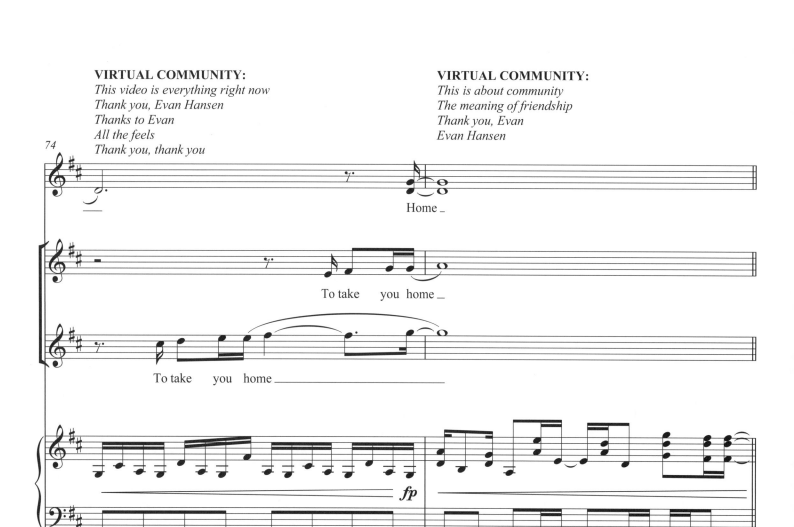

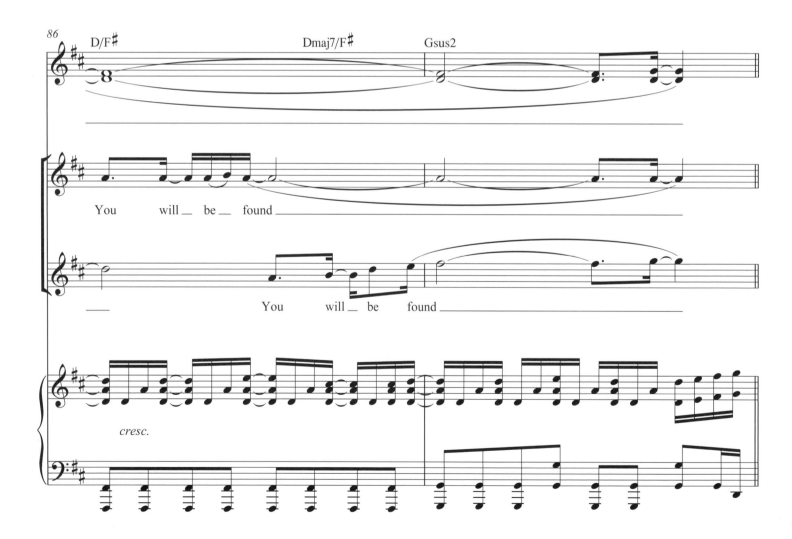

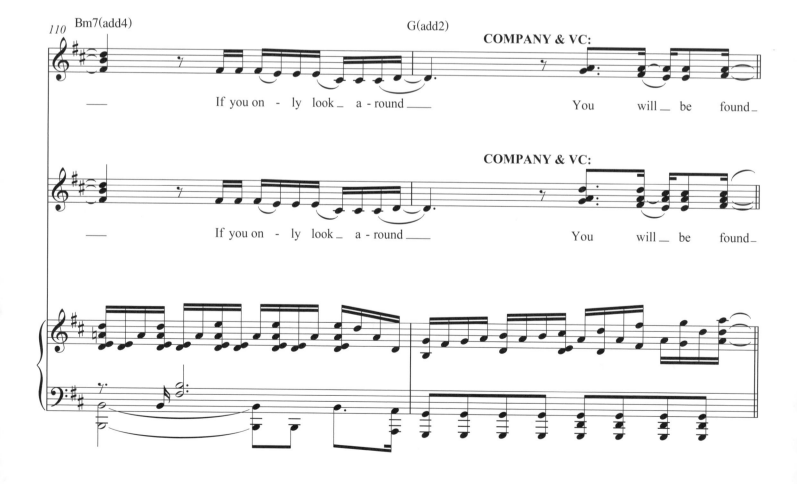

TO BREAK IN A GLOVE

Music and Lyrics by BENJ PASEK
and JUSTIN PAUL
Vocal arrangements by Justin Paul
Piano arrangement by
Alex Lacamoire and Justin Paul

EVAN: *This glove is really cool, wow.*
LARRY: *Why don't you take it?*
EVAN: *Oh no, I couldn't.*

LARRY: *Why not?*
EVAN: *Are you sure?*

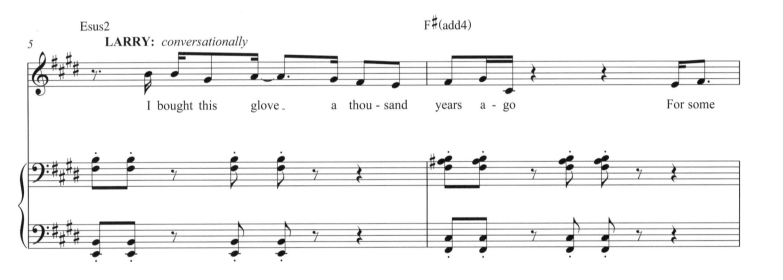

I bought this glove a thou-sand years a-go For some

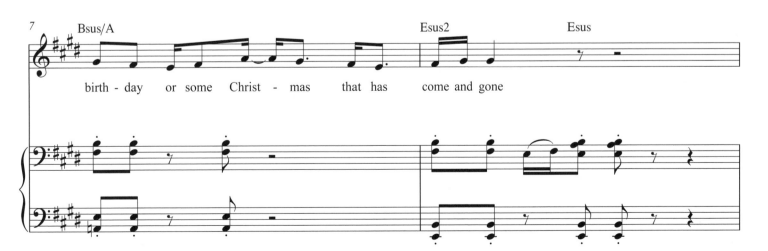

birth-day or some Christ-mas that has come and gone

I thought we might _ play catch or– I don't know But he left it in _ the bag _ with the tag _

_ still on

LARRY: *You'll have to break it in, though, first.*
You can't catch anything with it that stiff.

EVAN: *How do you break it in?*
LARRY: *Well...*

LARRY:
It's all a proc - ess that is rea - ly quite pre - cise A sort of

se - cret meth-od known _ to ver-y few So, if you're in the mar - ket for...

LARRY: *Shaving cream.*
EVAN: *Shaving cream?*
LARRY: *Oh yeah. You rub that in for about five minutes. Tie it all up with rubber bands, put it under your mattress, and sleep on it. And you do that for at least a week. Every day. Consistent.*

they can gloat_ a - bout_ the time_ they save_ 'Til they

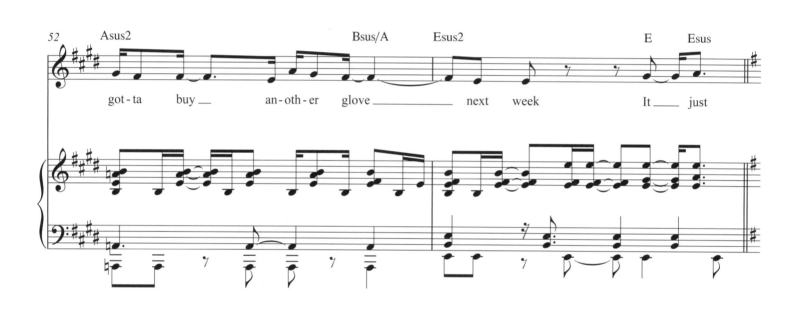

got - ta buy _ an-oth-er glove _____ next week It _ just

takes a lit - tle pa - tience It takes a lit - tle time ___

EVAN:

It takes a lit - tle pa - tience It takes a lit - tle time

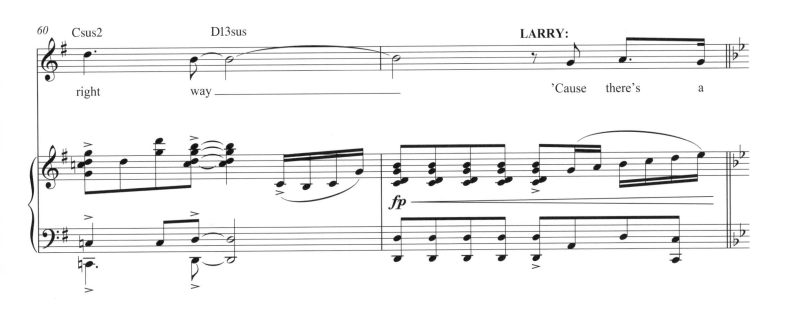

EVAN: *Connor was really lucky.*
To have a dad that...a dad who cared so much.
About...taking care of stuff.

LARRY: *Shaving cream. Rubber bands.*
Mattress. Repeat. Got it?
EVAN: *Got it.*

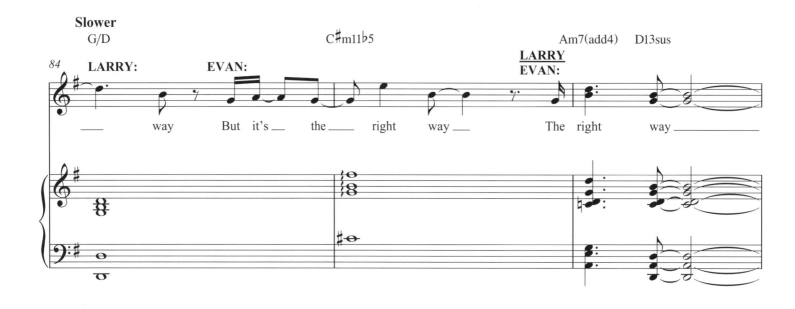

ONLY US

Music and Lyrics by BENJ PASEK
and JUSTIN PAUL
Vocal arrangements by Justin Paul
Piano arrangement by
Alex Lacamoire and Justin Paul

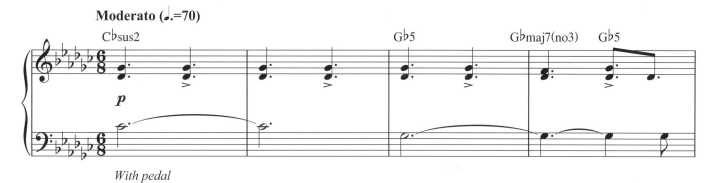

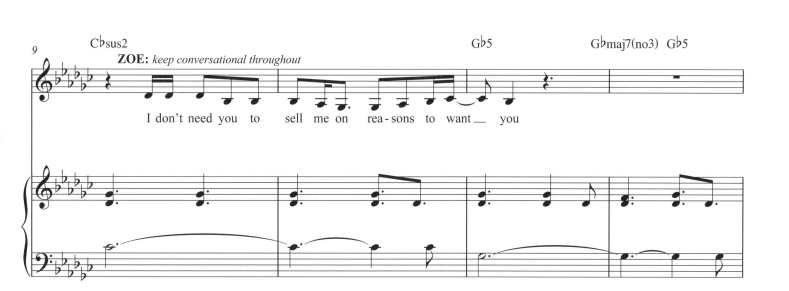

I don't need you to search_ for the proof_ that I _____ should

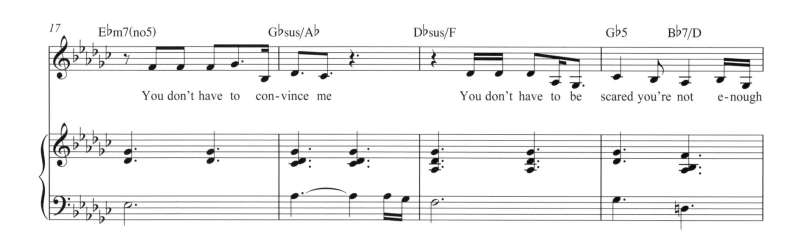

You don't have to con-vince me   You don't have to be   scared you're not   e-nough

'Cause what we've got go-in' __   is good

I don't need more re-mind - ers of all __ that's been __ bro - ken

GOOD FOR YOU

Music and Lyrics by BENJ PASEK
and JUSTIN PAUL
Vocal arrangements by Justin Paul
Piano arrangement by
Alex Lacamoire and Justin Paul

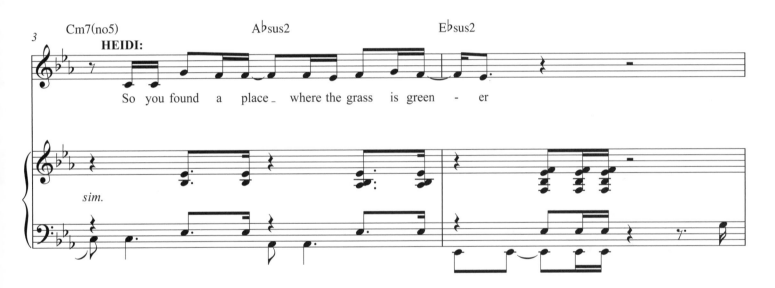

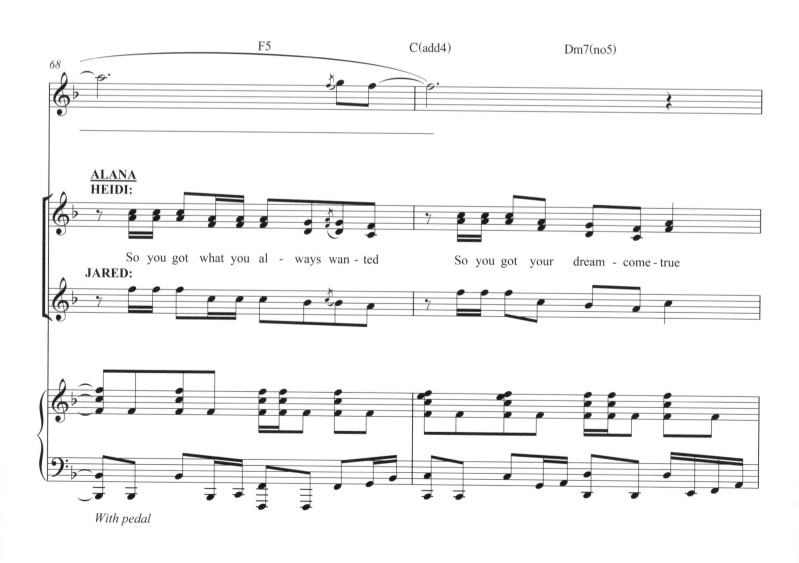

WORDS FAIL

Music and Lyrics by BENJ PASEK
and JUSTIN PAUL
Vocal arrangements by Justin Paul
Piano arrangement by
Alex Lacamoire and Justin Paul

Rubato, sempre colla voce

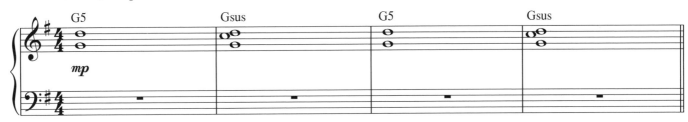

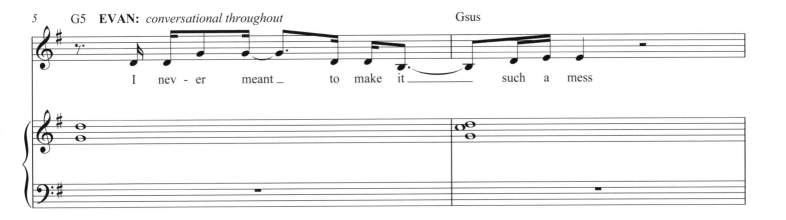

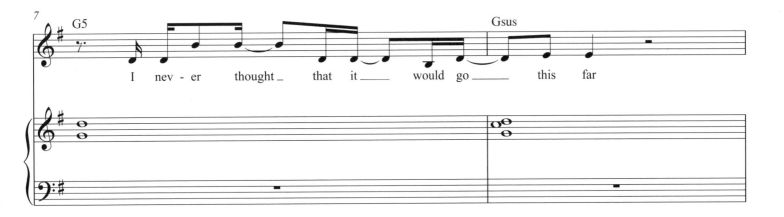

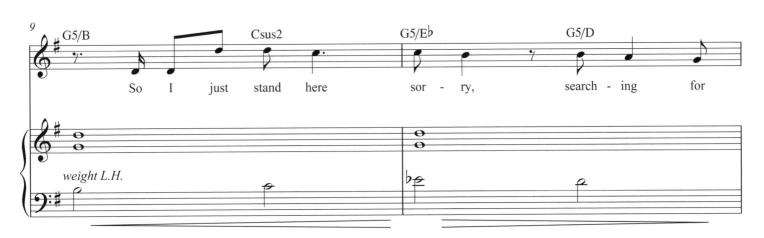

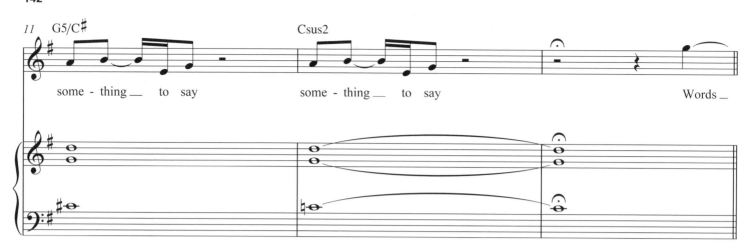

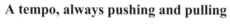

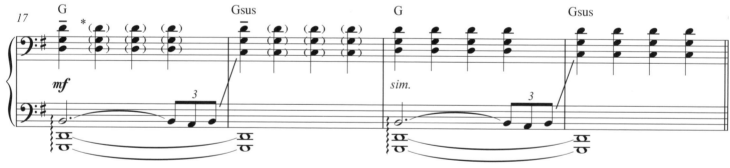

Notes in parentheses to be played quieter, like an echo.

No corn-y jokes or base-ball _____ gloves _____

No mom who ____ just ____ was there, _____ 'cause "Mom" was

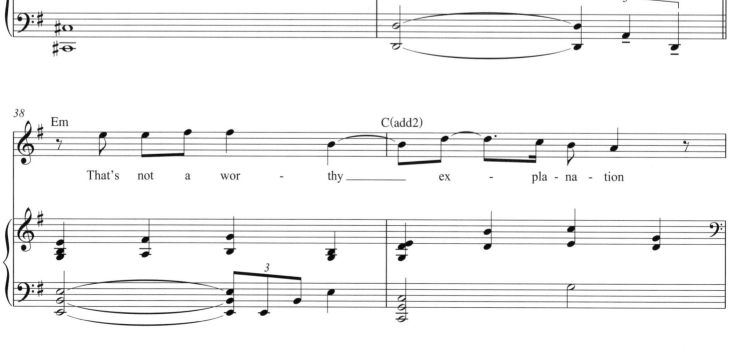

all that ____ she ____ had _____ to be ____

That's not a wor - thy _____ ex - pla - na - tion

146

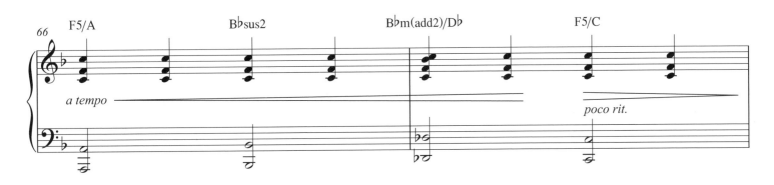

Rubato

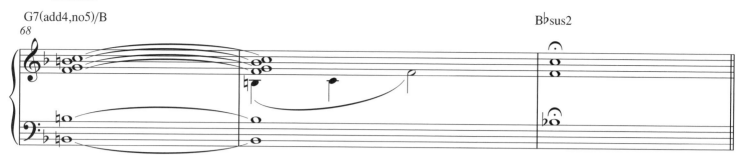

Colla voce

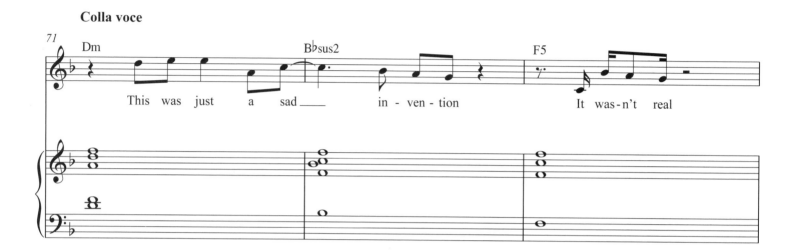

This was just a sad ___ in-ven-tion   It was-n't real

I ___ know   But we were hap-py   I guess I could-n't

Moderato (= 96)

let that go   I guess I could-n't give that up   I guess I want-ed to ___ be-lieve _

So how do I _____ step in, step in - to the sun? _

Moderato (♩=100)

_____ Step in - to the sun _

keep melody legato

rall.

SO BIG/SO SMALL

Music and Lyrics by BENJ PASEK
and JUSTIN PAUL
Vocal arrangements by Justin Paul
Piano arrangement by
Alex Lacamoire and Justin Paul

With rubato throughout, sempre colla voce

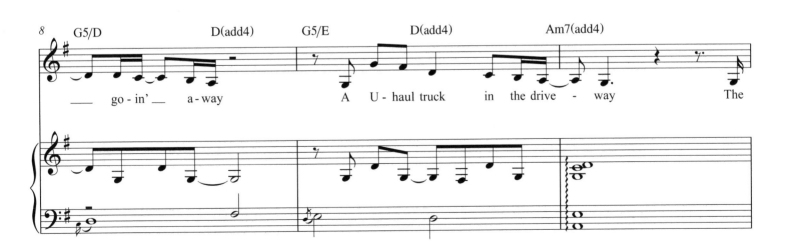

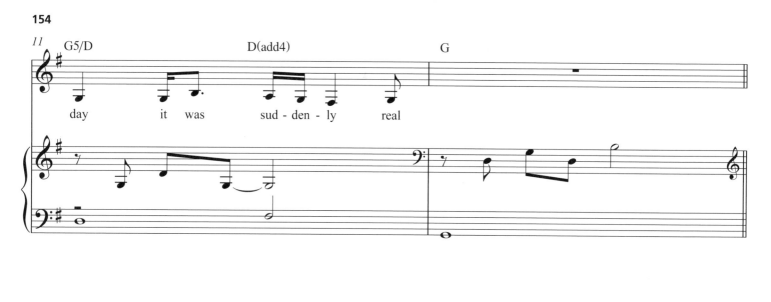

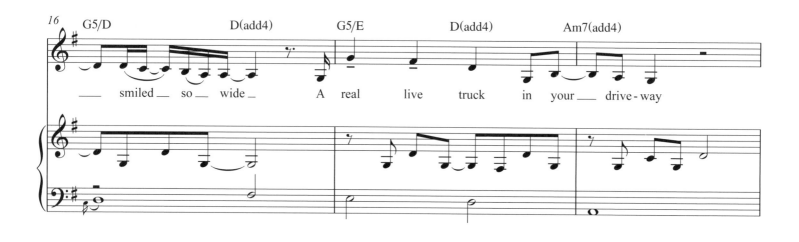

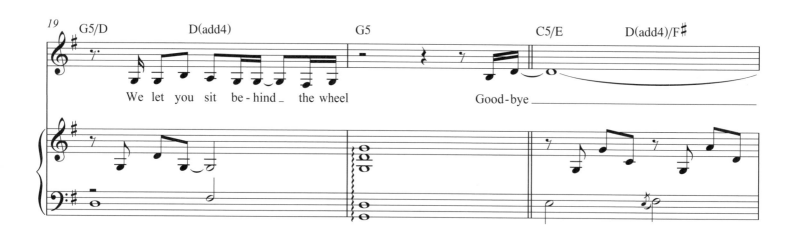

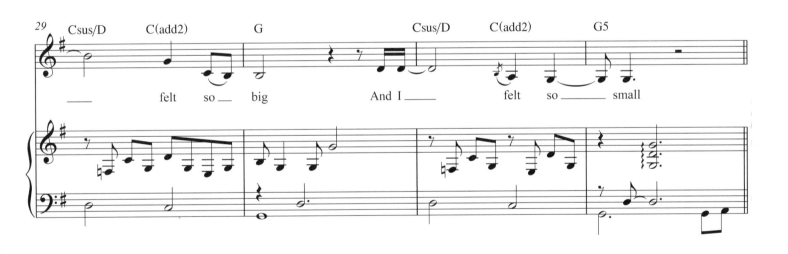

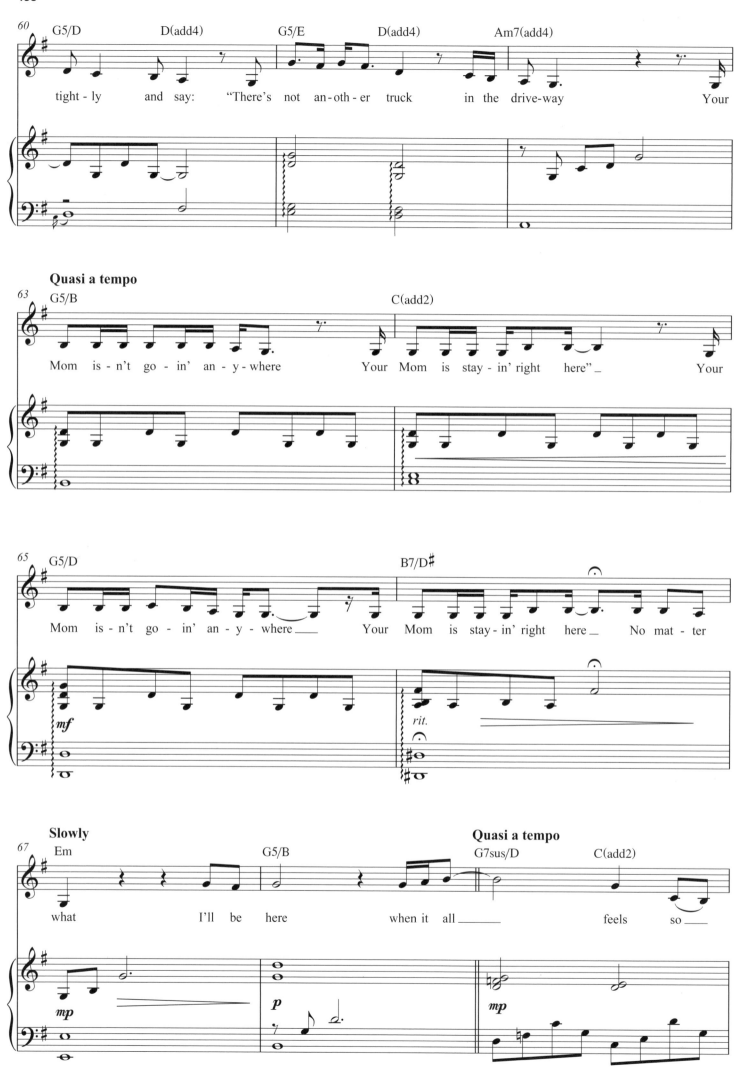